CHURCHES

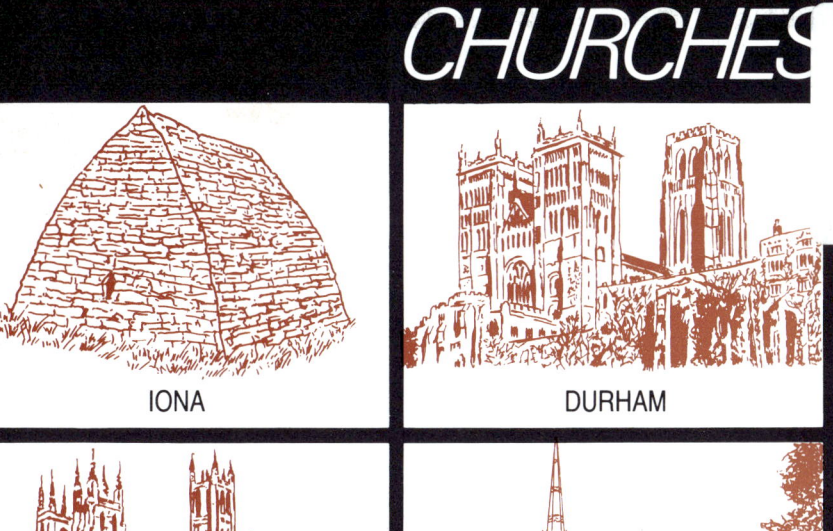

IONA	DURHAM	FOUNTAINS ABBEY
CANTERBURY	SALISBURY	YORK
ST DAVID'S	WESTMINSTER ABBEY	ST GEORGE'S CHAPEL
KING'S COLLEGE CHAPEL	ST PAUL'S	WESLEY'S CHAPEL
WESTMINSTER CATHEDRAL	COVENTRY	LIVERPOOL RC CATHEDRAL

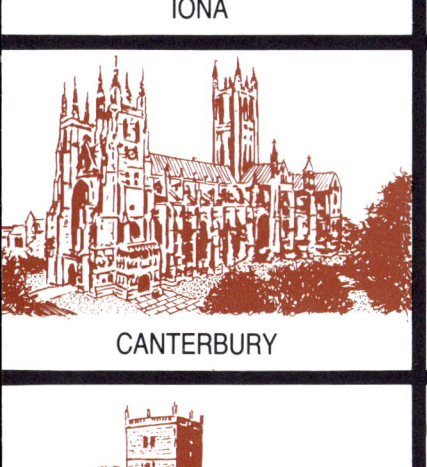

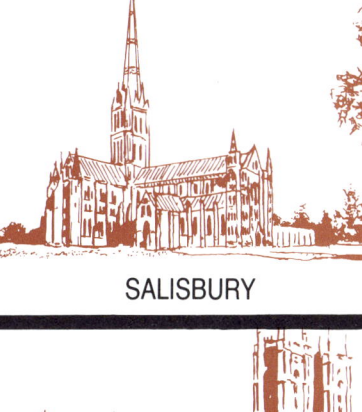

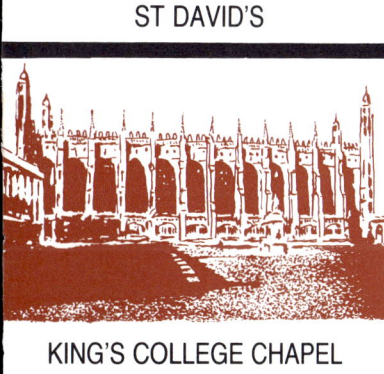

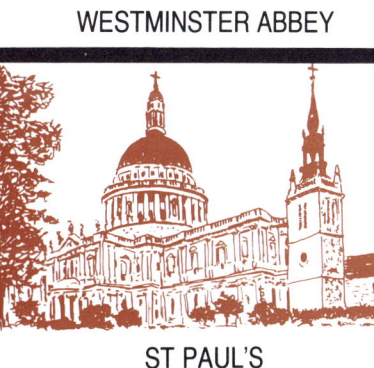

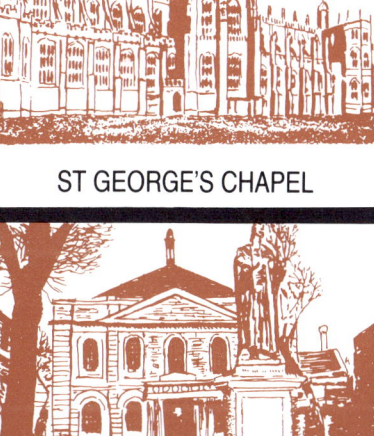

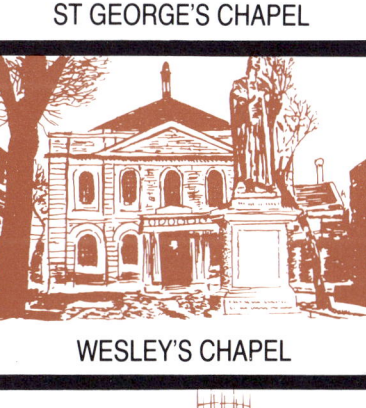

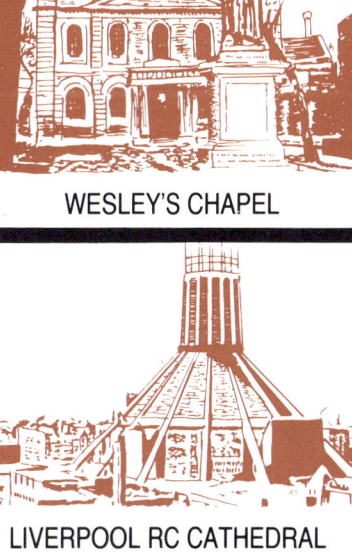

York Minster viewed from the old city walls

GREAT BRITISH CHURCHES

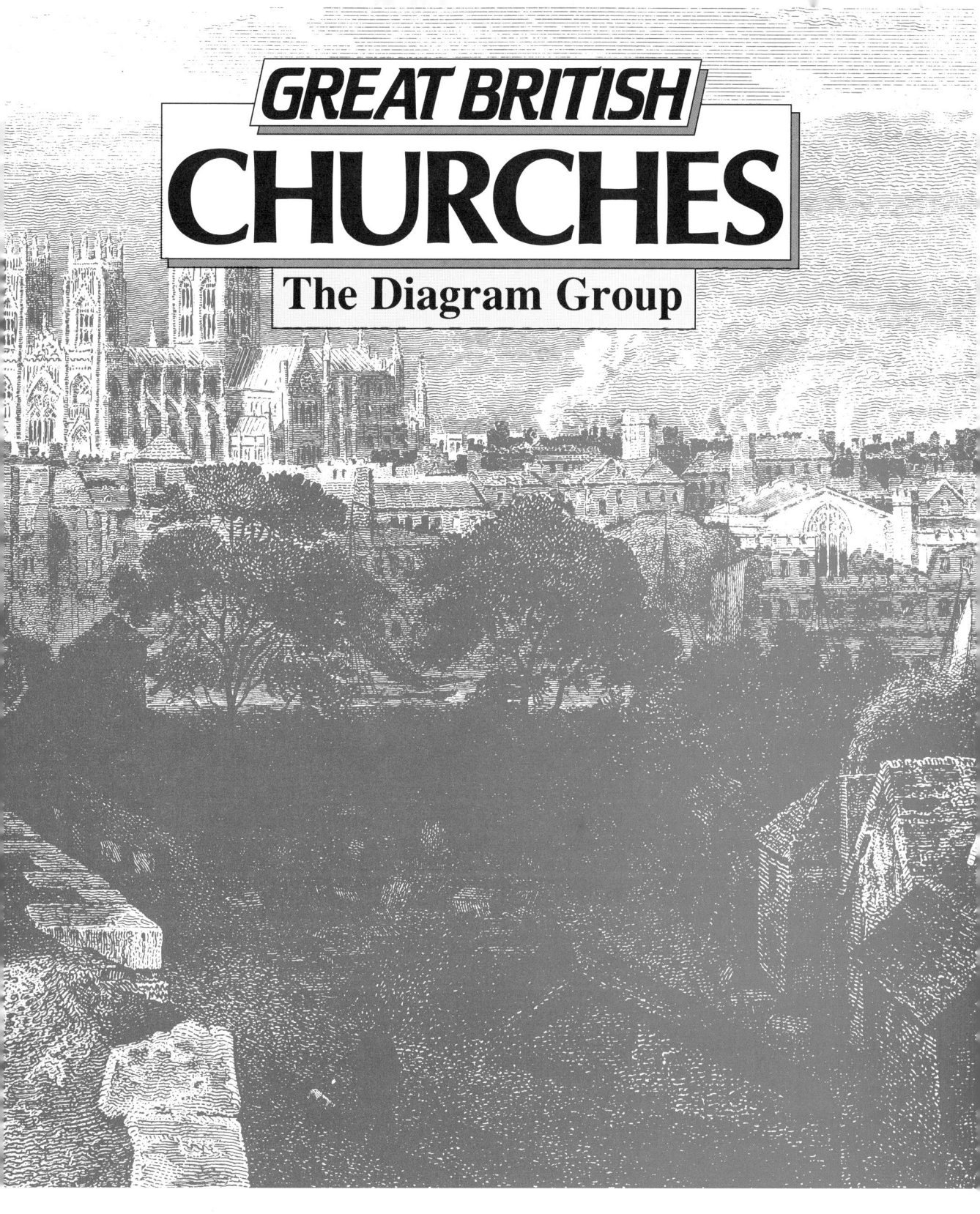

The Diagram Group

Franklin Watts
London New York Sydney Toronto

Acknowledgements
Picture Research: Patricia Robertson
Cover: British Tourist Authority
Title page: Mansell Collection
Architectural Press Ltd 35
BBC Hulton Picture Library 22
British Museum 13
British Tourist Authority 13 (bottom), 18, 31
John Lockie 9
Mansell Collection 11, 15, 17, 20, 21, 25, 26
National Trust for Scotland 7
John Rylands University Library of Manchester 28

Contents

The parts of a church	4
Iona	6
Durham Cathedral	8
Fountains Abbey	10
Canterbury Cathedral	12
Salisbury Cathedral	14
York Minster	16
St David's Cathedral	18
Westminster Abbey	20
St George's Chapel	22
King's College Chapel	24
St Paul's Cathedral	26
Wesley's Chapel	28
Westminster Cathedral	30
Coventry Cathedral	32
Metropolitan Cathedral Liverpool	34
Churches of interest	36
Things to look for in a church	38
Useful addresses	40
Index	41

© Diagram Visual Information Ltd 1987

First published in Great Britain 1987 by
Franklin Watts Ltd
12a Golden Square
London W1R 4BA

Printed in France

ISBN 0 86313 455 6

⁴ The parts of a church

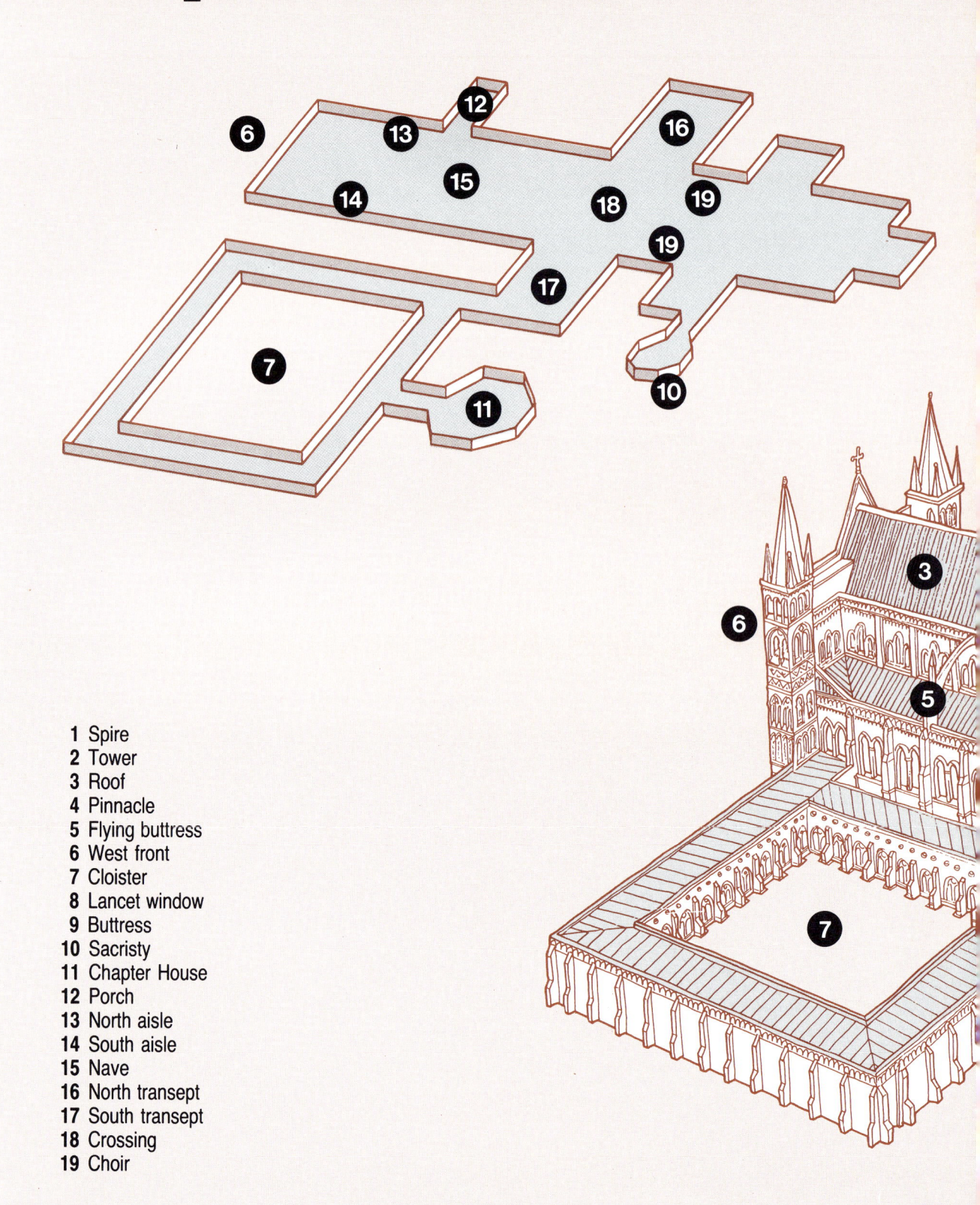

1 Spire
2 Tower
3 Roof
4 Pinnacle
5 Flying buttress
6 West front
7 Cloister
8 Lancet window
9 Buttress
10 Sacristy
11 Chapter House
12 Porch
13 North aisle
14 South aisle
15 Nave
16 North transept
17 South transept
18 Crossing
19 Choir

5

Iona

A reconstruction of a beehive-shaped cell in which St Columba and his monks lived.

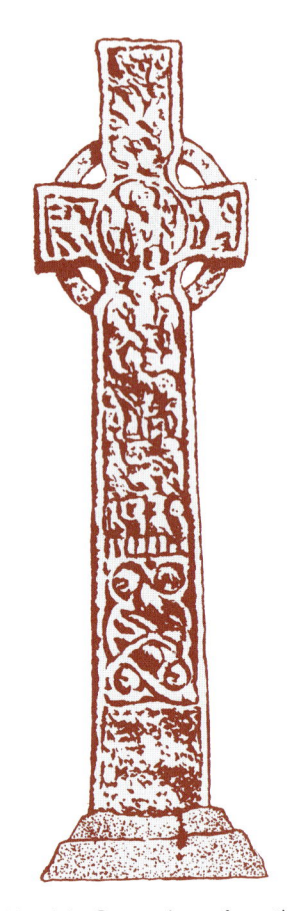

St Martin's Cross dates from the 10th century and is the only one left. This side has a Virgin and Child surrounded by four angels, with animals and groups of people on the shaft. The other side has bosses and serpents.

Iona is a small island about three miles long and one and a half miles wide off the north west coast of Scotland. It was a holy place even before Christianity when it was occupied by Druids. In AD 563 a scholarly Irish monk, Columba, came to Iona. He had founded several monasteries in Ireland and came with 12 followers to bring Christianity to the British people. Iona soon became the European centre of Christian learning and art.

The monastery Columba founded was simple. Each monk had a beehive-shaped cell or hut. Later an oak church, a mill, a barn and a stable were built and a refectory where visitors could eat. By the 7th century, Iona had become a place of pilgrimage. By the 9th century, it had become the traditional burial ground for the kings of Norway, Ireland and Scotland. About 60 kings are said to be buried there, including Duncan and Macbeth.

Iona was sacked several times by the Vikings.

They killed the monks and burned the buildings, but each time more pilgrims came. In 1072 Queen Margaret of Scotland ordered St Oran's Chapel to be built on the site of Columba's original church. It is now the oldest building on Iona.

In 1203 a Benedictine monastery was founded there. The abbey church became the cathedral of the bishop of the Isles. During the Reformation in 1560, when monasteries were closed down, the abbey buildings and hundreds of carved crosses were destroyed.

There is little left on Iona today from St Columba's time. In 1938 the Iona Community was founded. They restored the ruined abbey and live there as an experiment in Christian living. Each summer young people go there to share their way of life.

The rugged coast of Iona, with the Cathedral Church of St Mary in the distance.

563
Columba arrived on Iona
597
Columba died. Pilgrims began to come to Iona.
806
68 monks killed in Viking raid
1072
St Oran's Chapel built
1203
Benedictine abbey and monastery founded
1506
Abbey became cathedral of bishop of the Isles
1899
Iona given to the Church of Scotland by the Duke of Argyll
1912
Church reopened for services
1938
Iona Community founded. Excavation and restoration of abbey
1979
Acquired by National Trust for Scotland

Durham Cathedral

Durham Cathedral stands high on a rocky site almost entirely surrounded by a loop of the river Wear. It is dedicated to St Cuthbert, an extremely pious monk who was once a shepherd boy. He had been bishop of Lindisfarne and his body was brought to Durham by the monks who left Lindisfarne when Danish raids made it unsafe for them to live there. St Cuthbert had ordered that if the monks ever left there they should take his bones with them. He had died 200 years earlier but when the monks opened his coffin his body had not decayed.

The monks built the White Church which was used for almost a century. A new cathedral and abbey church of the Benedictines was begun in 1093. It was built remarkably quickly in 40 years. It is Britain's finest Norman cathedral and is visible for miles around. It has no west front, which most British cathedrals have, because it is so close to the river.

For centuries women were not allowed near St Cuthbert's shrine because he was reputed to be a woman hater. His shrine became one of the

The pectoral cross taken from St Cuthbert's coffin in 1827. It dates back to the 7th century and is of gold.

The remains of St Cuthbert's coffin, made in 698.

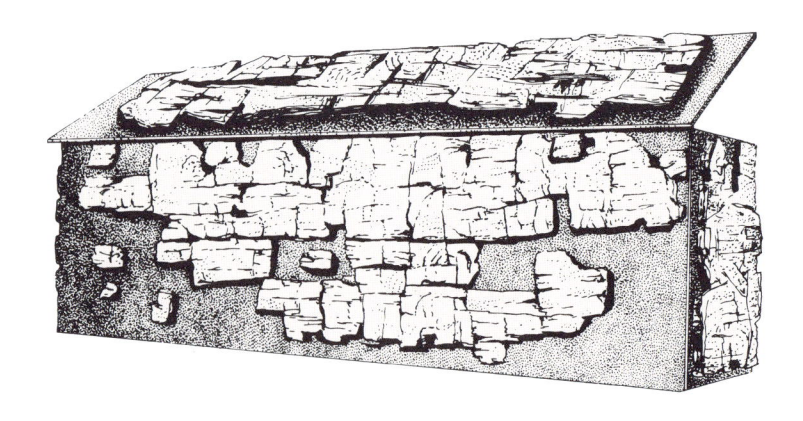

A replica of a Sanctuary Knocker. Any criminal reaching it could claim sanctuary in the cathedral until he was pardoned by the king.

The magnificent view of Durham Cathedral from the river side.

richest in England because of the many gifts of jewels. It was broken into by the king's agents in 1540 and many of the jewels were taken away. In 1650, the cathedral was used to house 4000 Scots prisoners taken by Oliver Cromwell. They stripped the cathedral of the choir stalls and anything that would burn to keep them warm.

By 1777 the building needed major repairs and parts of it were pulled down. Alterations to the cathedral began again in 1840 and continued for 30 years. Some of the original woodwork was taken down and is now in the university library. The cloisters and other monastic buildings were restored.

687
St Cuthbert died
998
White Church dedicated
1104
St Cuthbert's shrine finished
1133
Cathedral structure completed
c 1240
Chapel of Nine Altars completed
1262
Bell tower built
1540
Crown agents raided cathedral
1650
Cathedral damaged by prisoners
1777
Major repairs started
1840
Alterations made over next 30 years
1895
Chapter House rebuilt

Fountains Abbey

A reconstruction of the abbey.
1 Church
2 Cellarium - abbey storehouse
3 Kitchens
4 Refectory where monks ate
5 Hospice - guest house
6 Abbot's house
7 Monks' infirmary
8 Lay brothers' infirmary
9 Monks' dormitory

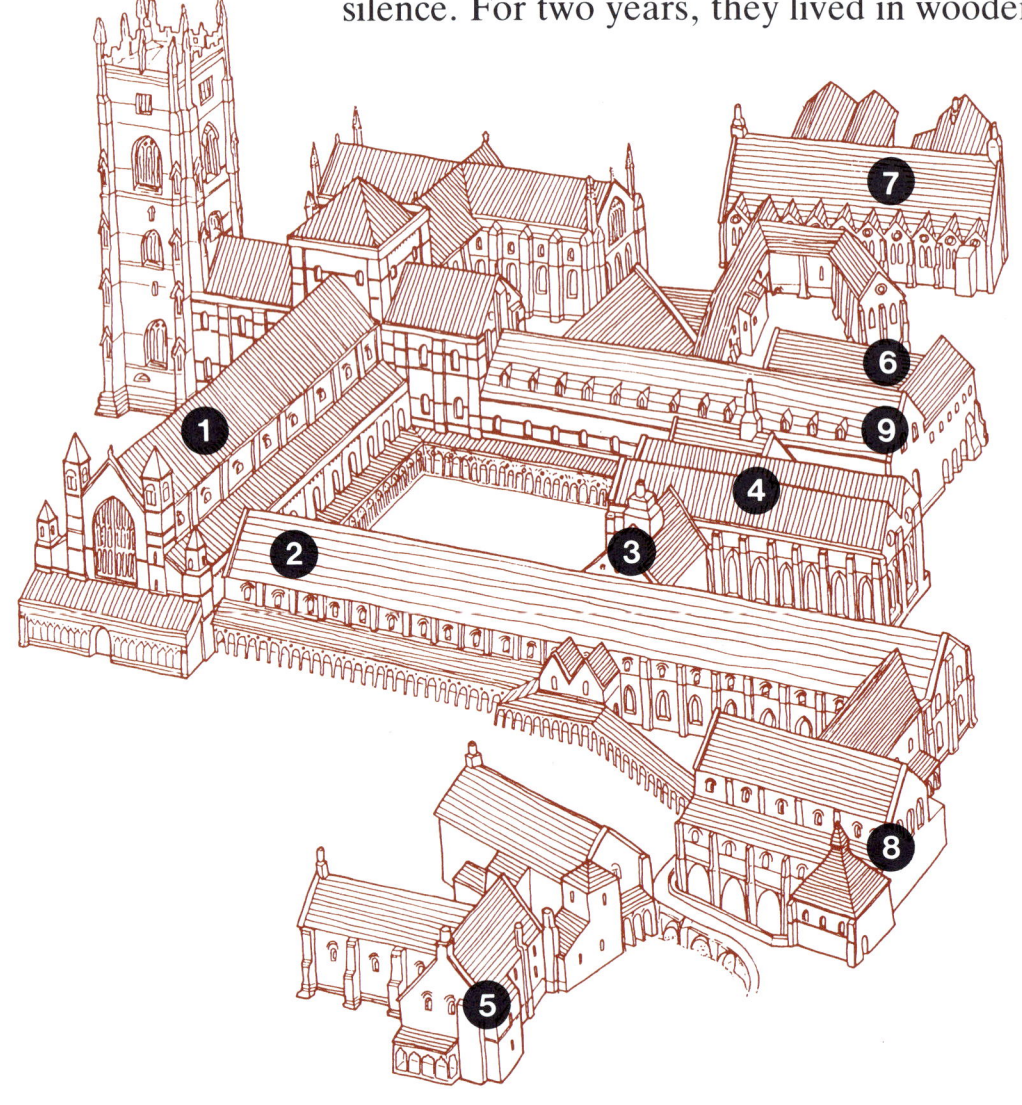

Fountains Abbey was founded by a band of 13 monks in 1132. They had left the Benedictine abbey of St Mary in York because they thought life was too easy and comfortable there. They settled in a remote part of Yorkshire, close to the river Skell. They called their abbey Fountains because of the clear springs in the area. The monks chose to become Cistercians, a more strictly religious order, and observed the rule of silence. For two years, they lived in wooden huts and had little to eat except boiled elm leaves because they had no income. The dean of York decided to retire to Fountains Abbey and brought with him his library and his wealth. Soon there were other gifts of land and money.

The monks were able to build a stone church. This was big enough for over 100 monks and several hundred lay brothers, who did the manual work, to pray together seven times a day. They built cloisters, for study, a dormitory and reredorter (a lavatory complete with running water and drains). They built a mill, a bakehouse and cellarium (storehouse). They also looked after the vast estates. Their sheep farms produced large quantities of wool and they had iron and lead mines. Fountains Abbey became the most powerful religious house in the north and the richest order in England.

Four hundred years of monastic life ended in 1539 when the State seized the wealth and property of the church during the Reformation. Lead was stripped from the roofs and stained glass and stones removed. The ruins of the medieval monastery of Fountains Abbey are the largest in Britain.

1132
Founded by monks from York
1135
First donations received
1138
Building in stone started
c1160
Most of abbey and monastery completed
1247
Chapel of Nine Altars added
1526
Tower added to church
1539
Abbey surrendered to Henry VIII
1611
Fountains Hall built from abbey stones
1720-40
Studley Royal park landscaped

The beautiful rural setting of the ruins of Fountains Abbey in the landscaped park of Studley Royal.

Canterbury Cathedral

Geoffrey Chaucer's *Canterbury Tales* told the stories of some of the pilgrims who came there. They were written in about 1387

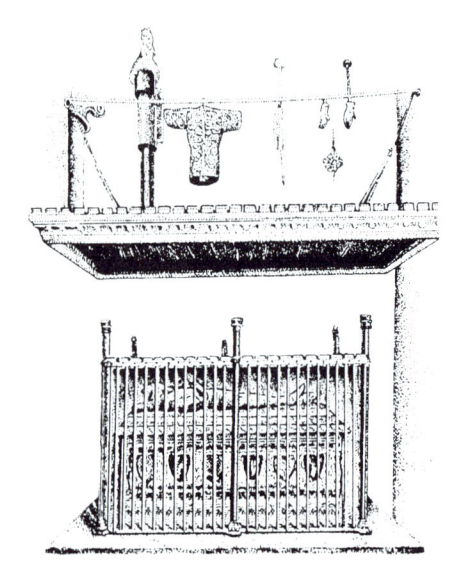

The tomb of Edward, the Black Prince. He was possibly called that because of his black armour. His overcoat, gauntlet, shield and scabbard hang above the tomb.

Canterbury Cathedral is the mother-church of the Anglican faith. It is the archbishop of Canterbury who crowns kings and queens in Westminster Abbey.

The original cathedral grew from a small church given to St Augustine in 597 by the Saxon King Ethelbert. It burned down in 1067. The first Norman archbishop, Lanfranc, ordered it to be rebuilt. This took only seven years.

The second cathedral was where Thomas Becket, archbishop of Canterbury, was killed by four knights after a quarrel with Henry II. Pilgrims from all over the world came to visit the martyr's shrine and brought many gifts. Henry II himself made a pilgrimage there. Canterbury became famous. It was the last staging post on the London to Dover road and, after Jerusalem and Rome, became the next chief place of pilgrimage.

Fire damaged the cathedral in 1174. The new cathedral was gradually rebuilt and included a bigger shrine to St Thomas Becket. William of Sens, a Frenchman, began the reconstruction. He fell from the scaffolding and William the Englishman carried on the work. Later additions included the great central tower, Bell Harry, which was completed in 1503. It is this cathedral that we see today.

In 1538, Becket's shrine was robbed and 26

cartloads of treasures were removed from the cathedral when Henry VIII closed down monasteries and seized church property. Three royal tombs have survived. Those of the Black Prince (died in 1376), Henry IV (died in 1413) and his queen, Joan of Navarre, who died in 1437. The cathedral also has some of the finest 13th-century stained glass and the largest crypt in England. It is one of Britain's best known and most visited cathedrals.

An early picture of the murder of Thomas Becket made in about 1200.

597
St Augustine arrived in Britain
1067
Cathedral burned down. Norman archbishop ordered rebuilding
1130
Choir consecrated
1170
Archbishop Thomas Becket killed
1173
Becket made saint by Pope Alexander III
1174
Henry II visited cathedral to do penance. Building damaged by fire
1175
Restoration work began
1468
North transept rebuilt
1503
Great central tower, Bell Harry, completed
1538
Cathedral attacked and robbed
1942
Cathedral survived bombing during Second World War

A view of Canterbury Cathedral. The West Front is on the left.

Salisbury Cathedral

The west front of the cathedral with the rows of saints just as 13th-century builders left it.

1219
Bishop Richard Poore received permission for new cathedral
1220
Foundations laid
1226
Lady Chapel completed
1256
Interior completed
1260
New Sarum dedicated
1270
Chapter house built
1284
Cloister built to connect chapter house with cathedral
1334
Master Richard of Farleigh designed spire
1450
Library built
1782-90
Many medieval features removed by James Wyatt from interior
1863
Interior restored by Sir George Gilbert Scott

Salisbury - or New Sarum - is the best example of a cathedral built in the English Gothic style. It was designed as a single unit by Canon Elias of Dereham. A plan of the cathedral appears at the front of this book.

Architects, as a rule, were hired to add to or modernise a building according to the latest style. Salisbury Cathedral, however, was not built by a series of architects over several centuries, like most English cathedrals. It was finished in only 40 years. The site chosen was in a peaceful Wiltshire valley. It was about a mile from where the old cathedral - Old Sarum - had stood for 150 years.

Master-mason Nicholas of Ely supervised the work. The Lady Chapel was completed in six years. After the main building was finished, an octagonal (eight-sided) chapter house for

An early view of the south west side showing the tallest spire in England.

administrative affairs was built. It has a thin central pillar to support a high, vaulted ceiling. A cloister (covered walkway) was also added. The spire, 123m (404ft) high, the tallest in England, was added later on top of the cathedral tower. It has survived for nearly 700 years but now needs frame braces to keep it in place.

The outside of the cathedral is very much as it was in the Middle Ages. The west front with its rows of saints is just as the 13th-century builders left it. The wall around the cathedral close still has medieval gateways. The interior of the cathedral has been altered several times. Over the years it has been filled with monuments and brasses. The library is a treasure house and contains one of the four original copies of the Magna Carta.

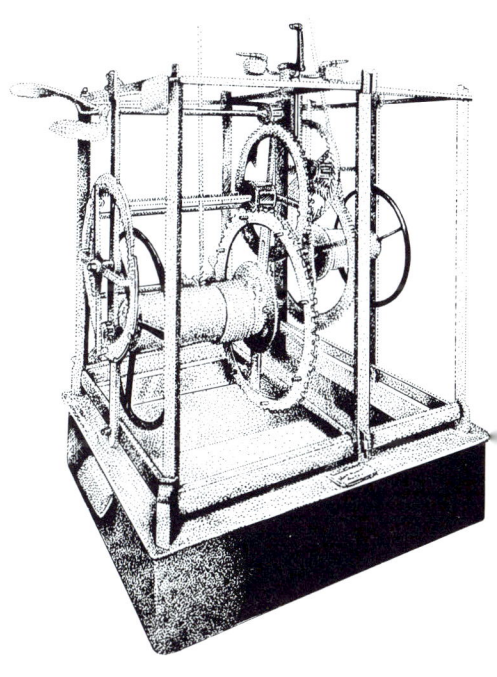

A 14th-century clock mechanism, at the west end of the north aisle. It still works and is believed to be the oldest in Europe.

York Minster

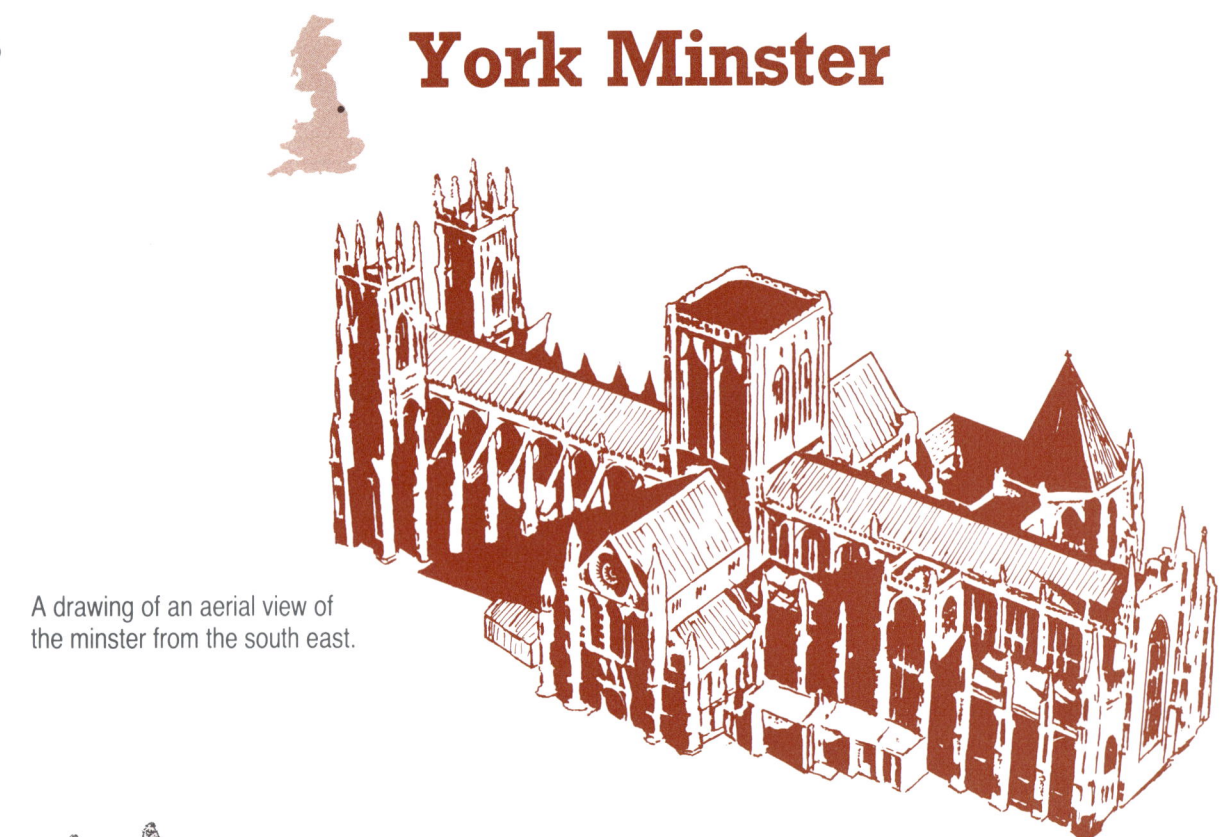

A drawing of an aerial view of the minster from the south east.

The tomb of Archbishop Walter de Gray who died in 1225. He began building the present minster.

There have been three important churches on the site of York Minster: a Saxon minster, a Norman cathedral and the medieval minster which is there today. Before that, there was a tiny wooden chapel, built for the baptism of Edwin, King of Northumbria, in 672. Earlier still, there was a Roman fortress which housed 5,600 soldiers of the Sixth Legion. In Roman times, York was already an important centre, known as Eboracum.

In Saxon Britain, in the early days of Christianity, a missionary centre was known as a minster and usually connected to a monastery. York was never a monastic church, but was a cathedral because it was the headquarters of a bishop and contained his cathedra or chair. From the Middle Ages, York Minster was also the seat of an archbishop. The archbishop of York was chief of the church in the north of England and second only to Canterbury.

The present minster is believed to have been commissioned in the 1220s by Archbishop Walter de Gray. He was a powerful figure in Henry III's government. The minster took 250 years to build and remains the largest medieval cathedral in Europe. It is 148m (486ft) long and 68m (223ft) across. It contains more original stained glass than any other church in Britain. Many of the windows have been taken out and carefully restored.

York Minster has had many problems caused by structural faults, fires and storms. In the mid-1960s the great central tower was in danger of collapse. It took five years to rebuild the foundations. In 1984, the minster was stuck by lightning and the roof of the south transept was destroyed by fire.

The choir screen was built between 1475-1500. It has statues of all the kings of England from William the Conqueror to Henry VI.

627
First wooden chapel built
1070
Norman cathedral begun
c1220
Present minster begun
1407
Central tower collapsed; rebuilt 30 years later
1472
Rededication of minster
1472-1500
Choir screen with statues of kings built
1829
Fire damaged minster
1938
New High Altar designed
1984
Roof of south transept damaged by fire

St David's Cathedral

St David's is in a valley on the most western tip of Wales and is the oldest cathedral settlement in Britain. It is not much more than a village in size but is a city because of the cathedral. It was founded by a bishop-abbot in the 6th century. He became St David, or Dewi Sant, the patron saint of Wales. His death on 1st March is remembered as St David's Day.

The monastery which St David founded became famous as a centre of learning and became a place of pilgrimage. William the Conqueror visited there in 1081. Henry II also came to St David's, trying to make amends for his part in the murder of St Thomas Becket in Canterbury Cathedral. The pilgrims brought so many gifts that the monks were able to start building a new cathedral in 1180.

Work on the cathedral went on for three centuries. It was the biggest and most ambitious

St David, patron saint of Wales. The dove on his shoulder is the legendary symbol of his eloquence at a 6th-century church meeting.

A view of St David's Cathedral from the south east.

building ever attempted in Wales. Craftsmen were brought in from the west of England, and sandstone to add to the purplish-grey stone quarried from the sea cliffs nearby. There were many setbacks. In 1220 a new tower collapsed. This was quite common in building periods of that time. An earth tremor caused damage in 1248. There was much building and rebuilding when things went wrong. By 1509 the cathedral seemed complete.

After the Reformation, when monasteries were closed down, the bishop's palace was no longer needed to entertain important pilgrims. During the 17th and 18th centuries the buildings fell into ruins. John Nash designed a new west front but this was replaced. Restoration work began again and Sir George Gilbert Scott based his design on the original 12th-century work.

The Bishop's Throne is the work of several periods. It has three elaborate canopies. It dates from about 1500.

One of the misericords under the choir stalls. They jutted out a little and gave some support when the stalls were pushed up during periods of standing. The misericords often had humorous carvings.

6th century
Settlement founded by St David
1081
Visit by William the Conqueror
1171
Visit by Henry II
1180
Present cathedral begun
1220
Central tower collapsed
1248
Damaged by earth tremor
1275
St David's shrine completed
1284
Visit by Edward I
1793
Restoration by John Nash
1860
Restoration by Sir George Gilbert Scott
1955
Visit by HM the Queen

Westminster Abbey

A view of the west towers of the Abbey. Big Ben and the Houses of Parliament can be seen to the left.

1065
Abbey consecrated
1066
William the Conqueror crowned
1245
Rebuilding of abbey begun by Henry III
1272
Building stopped
1300
Coronation chair made
1376
Building started again
1503-19
Henry VII's Chapel built
1540
Monastery closed. Abbey became cathedral for 10 years
1560
Abbey became royal collegiate church
1745
West towers completed
1920
Unknown warrior buried in tomb
1953
Coronation of HM Queen Elizabeth II

Almost every English monarch from William the Conqueror to Queen Elizabeth II has been crowned in Westminster Abbey. It is not a cathedral, but a church. Its proper name is the Royal Collegiate Church of St Peter of Westminster.

The first Westminster Abbey was founded by Edward the Confessor. It was finished a few days before his death in 1065. William the Conqueror was crowned there the following year, after his victory at the Battle of Hastings. The abbey was then a church and a monastery on an island in the river Thames. It lasted for 200 years.

Henry III had the abbey pulled down. He wanted a bigger and better abbey, more suitable for coronations. Work began in 1245 but stopped when he died. Building began again in the 14th century. Progress was slow. The western end of the nave was finished in the 15th century. Two

Poets' Corner has many statues and memorials to famous people. Like Shakespeare, Milton and Wordsworth, not all are buried here.

later additions were the magnificent Henry VII's Chapel, completed in 1519, and the west towers which were not finished until 1745.

When monasteries were closed down, the abbey became a cathedral, but only for 10 years. In 1560, in the reign of Queen Elizabeth I, it became a royal church, responsible directly to the Crown. Many monarchs have been married and buried in Westminster Abbey.

There are memorials and tombs of some of the greatest poets, authors, playwrights, musicians, scientists, statesmen and soldiers. The simplest is the Tomb of the Unknown Warrior, a memorial to all soldiers who have died for the country. Westminster Abbey is the setting for many ceremonial services and occasions. It is a historic monument but ordinary church services are still held there as often as possible.

The Coronation Chair was made for Edward I. Under the seat is the Stone of Scone which was the coronation seat of many early Scottish kings. Since 1308 all the sovereigns of England, except Edward V and Edward VIII, have been crowned on this chair.

St George's Chapel

The sovereign and knights leaving the chapel after the service for the Knights of the Garter.

The star of the Most Noble Order of the Garter.

St George's Chapel is situated within the walls of Windsor Castle. The Royal Family traditionally celebrates Matins, the service of morning prayer, on Christmas morning there. It is a 'royal peculiar' - a church which comes under the control of the sovereign, not a bishop.

The first chapel was built in the 13th century by Henry III. His great-grandson, Edward III, gave the chapel a greater importance. He founded the Most Noble Order of the Garter in 1348. It was the highest order of chivalry in England. The total number was 26, including the sovereign.

The present chapel was begun by Edward IV in 1475. He wanted a more glorious royal church after his victories abroad. Building started slowly and, when he died, he was buried in the still unfinished chapel. Building continued under

The west front with the main entrance to St George's Chapel.

Henry VII and was finished under the reign of Henry VIII.

St George's Chapel is famous as the chapel of the Knights of the Order of the Garter. The original chapel of the Order is now the Albert Memorial Chapel. Queen Victoria had it converted and it is a fine example of Victorian workmanship. The Garter Service is usually held each year in June. The banners, crested helmets and heraldic plates of the past and present knights are hung above the choir stalls. It is the best display of heraldry in the country. The royal pews are separate from the knights' and the sovereign's is marked by the royal standard.

St George's Chapel is also a royal burial place. Since George III, every monarch and other members of the royal families have tombs there.

1240
Henry III built first chapel
1348
Order of the Garter founded
1351
Chapel became a 'royal peculiar'
1475
St George's Chapel begun
1484
Choir and chancel completed
1528
Chapel completed
1643-60
Buildings damaged during Civil War
1782-92
Chapel restored by George III
1948
Celebrations to mark 600th anniversary of Order of the Garter
1969
King George VI Memorial Chapel completed

King's College Chapel

King's College Chapel is one of Britain's finest examples of perpendicular architecture. It has tall spires, huge buttresses and perfect fan vaulting. It is often compared with St George's Chapel at Windsor and Henry VII's Chapel in Westminster Abbey. The chapel is the best-known of Cambridge's many notable buildings and has inspired many painters and poets.

King's College Chapel was named after Henry VI. It was originally part of a scheme for a new college. It was a dual foundation with Eton College, the public school, from where it used to take scholars. The plan was for a huge chapel, joined to an arcaded court, and a bell tower near the river. The foundation stone was laid in 1446 but progress was slow because of lack of money. Political unrest led to the Wars of the Roses and Henry VI was deposed. His successors provided money for the building of the chapel and the fan-vaulted ceiling was built during the reign of Henry VII. It looks spectacular but it does not support the roof itself. There is a timber frame to support it. The stained glass and large carved oak organ screen were added by Henry VIII. The chapel building was completed in 1536, 90 years after Henry VI laid the foundation stone. The plan of the chapel is simple but it is richly decorated. In 1960 the east end was altered so it could hold the most expensive painting sold at auction at that time. This was Rubens' The Adoration of the Magi.

In the 17th century a musical tradition was started. The Festival of Nine Lessons and Carols sung by the choir of King's College Chapel on Christmas Eve is now televised worldwide.

A view from the south showing the perpendicular architecture

1446
Foundation stone laid by Henry VI
1461
Building stopped
1515
Structure completed
1517-31
Flemish glaziers worked on windows
1536
Chapel ready for use
1873
Non-Etonians admitted to King's College for first time
1960s
East end of chapel remodelled

The interior of the chapel showing the beautiful fan-vaulted ceiling.

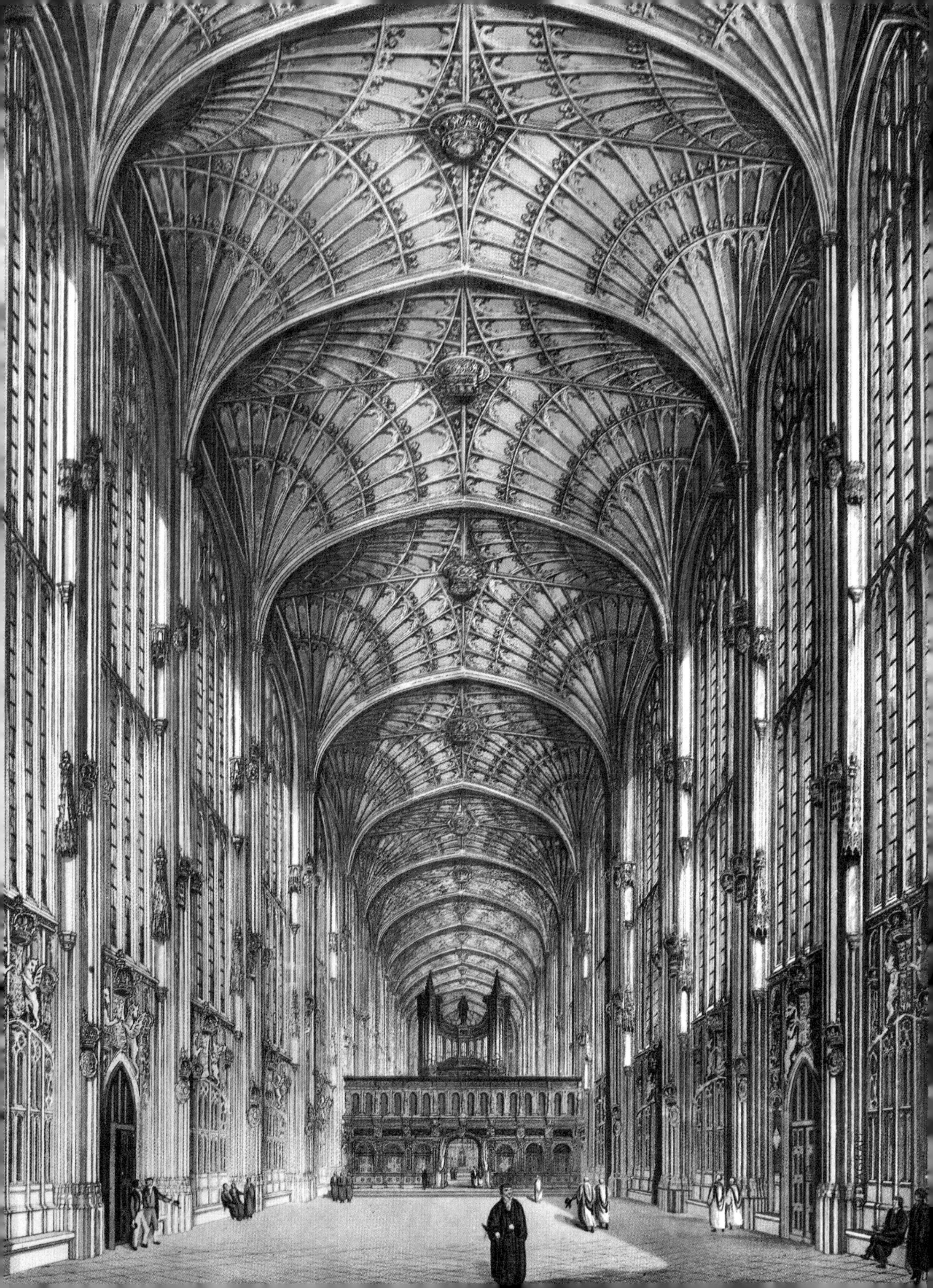

St Paul's Cathedral

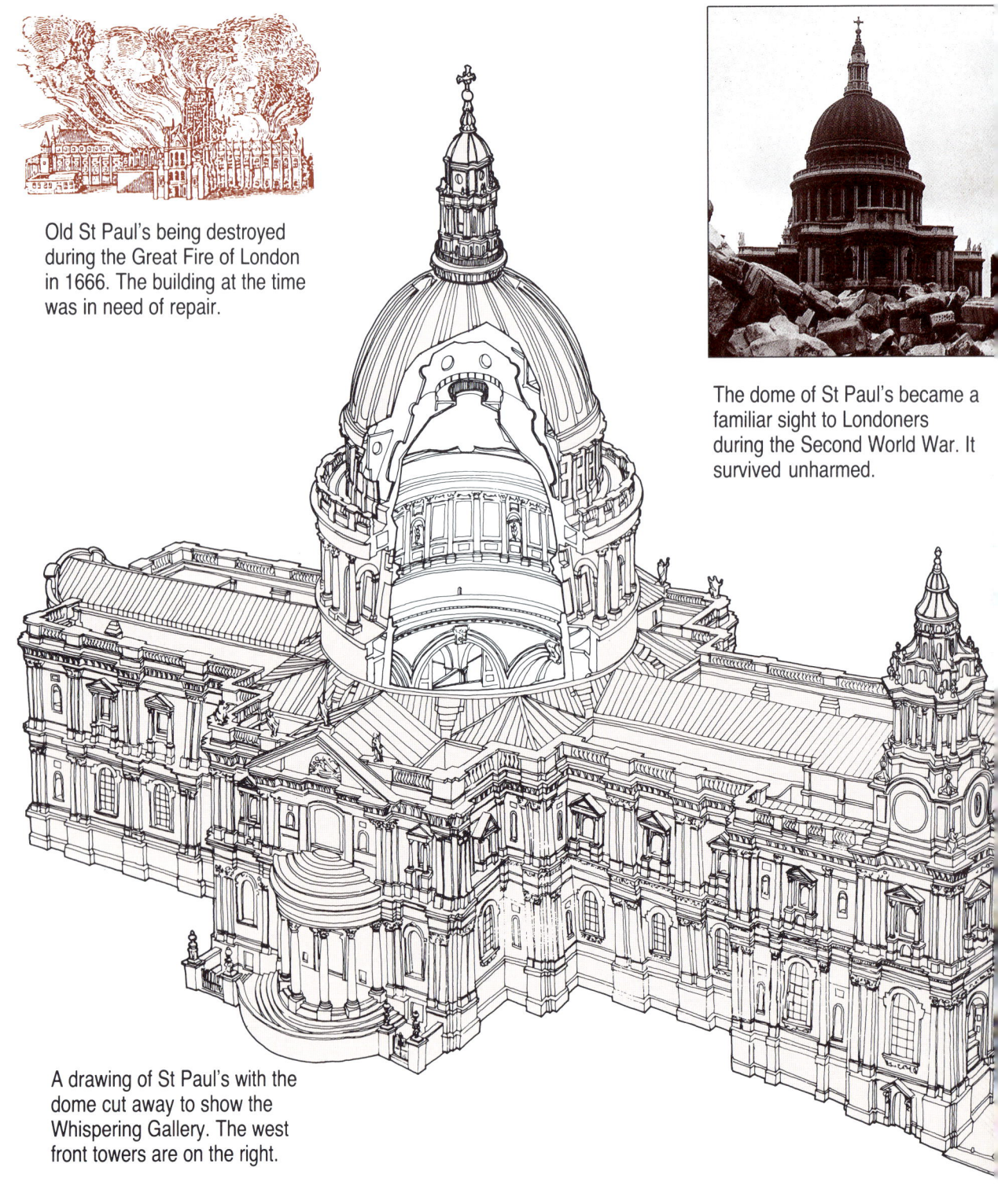

Old St Paul's being destroyed during the Great Fire of London in 1666. The building at the time was in need of repair.

The dome of St Paul's became a familiar sight to Londoners during the Second World War. It survived unharmed.

A drawing of St Paul's with the dome cut away to show the Whispering Gallery. The west front towers are on the right.

604
First cathedral founded
1240
Old St Paul's completed
1666
Old St Paul's destroyed in Great Fire of London
1675
Work started on new St Paul's
1708
New St Paul's completed
1723
Sir Christopher Wren died, aged 91
1897
Thanksgiving Service for Queen Victoria's Diamond Jubilee
1940
Cathedral damaged in Blitz
1965
State Funeral of Sir Winston Churchill
1981
Marriage of Prince Charles and Lady Diana Spencer

A cathedral dedicated to St Paul has stood on the same site in London since 604. It is the mother church of the diocese of London. Unlike most cathedrals, it takes its name from its saint and not the place where it is situated like Canterbury or Salisbury. The first cathedral was burned down. The second sacked by Vikings, the third was also burned down and the fourth was destroyed in the Great Fire of London in 1666.

Christopher Wren designed the present cathedral. It was his third design because the first two were turned down. It is the only cathedral with a dome and it was built in only 35 years under his supervision. Money for it was raised by a tax on coal coming into the Port of London.

Wren's design was based on the Latin cross, with a huge dome. This weighs 64,000 tons and rises 111m (364ft) above the ground. The best place to see the paintings in the dome of the life of St Paul by James Thornhill is from the Whispering Gallery. A whisper can be heard from the other side of the gallery about 31m (100ft) away. You have to climb 650 steps to get there. The dome was not damaged during the bombing of London in the Second World War. Other parts of the cathedral were badly damaged. They were all restored and a new High Altar was added in 1958.

The crypt is one of the largest in the world. There are many memorials and tombs there. Sir Christopher Wren is buried there, so are Admiral Horatio Nelson and the Duke of Wellington.

As it is the cathedral of the capital, it is the centre of many national occasions and ceremonies. It needs 130 people, clergy and lay people, to run it. It is the most visited cathedral in England.

Wesley's Chapel

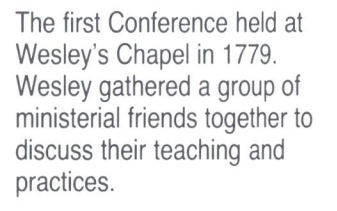

The first Conference held at Wesley's Chapel in 1779. Wesley gathered a group of ministerial friends together to discuss their teaching and practices.

John Wesley walking between two friends in Edinburgh in 1790. By this time he was an old man and died the following year.

Wesley's Chapel in the city of London is the mother church of Methodism. It was founded by John Wesley. He went to Oxford University and planned his day so no time was wasted. His friends copied his methods and they became known as the Methodists.

When John started preaching as a Church of England clergyman, his sermons made people feel uncomfortable. He felt the church was not doing enough to help the poor and needy. He was banned from preaching in an Anglican church so he started preaching outdoors. Throughout England and Wales many places are still marked with a plaque where John Wesley stopped to preach.

For his first Methodist chapel, John converted a gun foundry in the city of London. It was not only a place of prayer but it became a medical centre for the poor. In those days, medical care was very expensive. This chapel lasted for 40 years but became too expensive to repair. He decided to build a new chapel nearby. Foundations were laid in 1777. King George III gave ships' masts to be used as pillars and Methodists all over England donated money for the building and furnishing.

The chapel looks today much as it did 200 years ago. It was damaged by fire in 1879 but was completely restored. In 1891 a bronze statue of John Wesley was put in the forecourt to commemorate his death a hundred years earlier. By 1972 the chapel was in urgent need of repair and money was raised by Methodists all over the world for this. On 1st November 1978, the Queen and Prince Philip attended a service to celebrate the reopening of the chapel.

The chapel in City Road, London, was built in 1778. There is now a statue of John Wesley in the forecourt.

28 June 1703
John Wesley born in Epworth, Lincolnshire
1739
Wesley bought disused foundry
1746
Began free medical clinic for the poor
1748
Opened refuge for widows and orphans
1777
Foundation stone of new chapel laid
1778
First service held in chapel
1791
John Wesley died
1879
Chapel damaged by fire
1972
Chapel declared unsafe. Restoration begun
1978
HM Queen Elizabeth II attended reopening service

Westminster Cathedral

Westminster Cathedral is the headquarters of the Roman Catholic faith in Britain. In the early 19th century, a law was passed which allowed English Catholics to practise again. This was almost three centuries after Henry VIII had broken with the church of Rome and closed down monasteries. The first Roman Catholic archbishop of Westminster was elected in 1850.

Cardinal Wiseman did not have a cathedral. His successor, Cardinal Manning, bought the land on which the cathedral stands. It used to be a fairground and site of a prison. The third archbishop, Cardinal Vaughan, laid the first stone in 1895. The cathedral took only seven years to build but he and the architect, John Francis Bentley, died before it was finished.

The striking and unusual exterior of Westminster Cathedral with the slender bell tower.

The cathedral is very different from traditional cathedrals. The founder and architect chose not to build in the Gothic style for two reasons. It was too expensive and they did not want it to look like Westminster Abbey nearby. The style of the cathedral is early Christian Byzantine so it is more eastern Mediterranean than English. It was built with 12 million bricks with layers of Portland stone in between, and there is no steel reinforcement.

The interior of the cathedral was left unfinished so future generations could add to the decoration. The plan was that the walls should be covered with marble to a height of about 9m (30ft) with mosaics above that. So far over 100 different kinds of marble from all over the world have been used and there are many exotic mosaics.

The bronze statue of St Peter, the patron saint of Westminster. It is a copy of the statue in St Peter's in Rome.

1884
Site for cathedral purchased
1895
Foundation stone laid
1896
Foundations completed
1903
Structure completed. First mass held in Chapel of Our Lady
1910
Cathedral consecrated. A single bell hung in bell tower
1929
Mass marking centenary of Catholic freedom to worship in England
1976
Pedestrian piazza in front of cathedral provided by Church of England

An example of some of the superb mosaics to be found in the interior of the cathedral.

Coventry Cathedral

Coventry Cathedral showing the old and the new.

1 The ruins of the Cathedral of St Michael. The 15th-century spire survived.

2 St Michael's Porch with a massive oak cross is the entrance to the new cathedral.

3 Sir Jacob Epstein's sculpture of St Michael defeating the devil.

4 The Baptistry Window, designed by John Piper and made by Patrick Reyntiens.

5 The nave windows were the gifts of many people.

6 The Chapel of Christ the Servant (also called the Chapel of Industry) is joined to the cathedral by a wide corridor.

The present cathedral is the third in Coventry and is both ancient and modern. The first cathedral served the Benedictine monastery founded by Earl Leofric and his wife, Lady Godiva. She was famous for riding naked through the streets on horseback in protest against the heavy taxes her husband put on the town. It was destroyed in 1538 when monasteries were closed under Henry VIII. The second cathedral of St Michael was destroyed during an air raid in 1940.

A competition was held for a design for the new cathedral. It was won by Basil Spence. Work began in 1954 and the cathedral was finished in 1962. It has attracted many visitors for there is much to see. Sir Basil Spence preserved the ruins of the old church and made a paved open forecourt leading from the old to the new cathedral. Two of the most moving relics are the

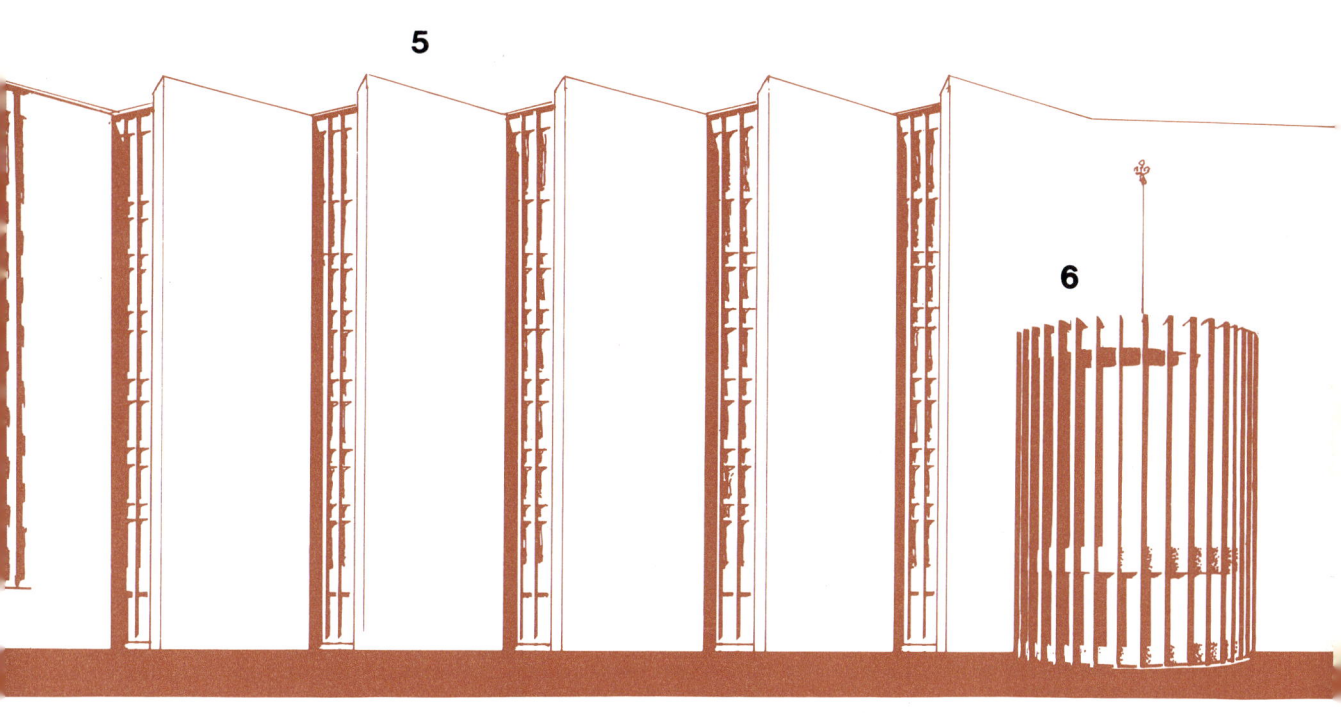

Charred Cross, made from two blackened roof beams, which stands in the sanctuary of the ruins, and the Cross of Nails, made from 14th-century hand-forged nails which fell from the roof.

The interior of the cathedral is magnificent. Over the High Altar is the world's largest tapestry, designed by Graham Sutherland. It took 30,000 hours to make. John Piper designed the Baptistry Window, which is a blaze of colour from floor to ceiling. The font is a huge boulder which comes from a hillside near Bethlehem. The west screen is clear glass engraved by John Hutton, and many of the stained glass windows and mosaic floors have been the gifts from people all over the world. A bronze sculpture by Sir Jacob Epstein of St Michael defeating the devil is on the wall outside the main entrance.

1043
First church, later to become cathedral, built
1373
Work began on second cathedral church of St Michael
1918
Church of St Michael became cathedral
1940
Cathedral destroyed by fire bombs
1951
Sir Basil Spence won competition to design new cathedral
1954
Reconstruction of new cathedral begun
1960
Font installed
1962
Coventry Cathedral consecrated in presence of HM Queen Elizabeth II

Metropolitan Cathedral Liverpool

A model of the original domed cathedral designed by Sir Edwin Lutyens to contrast with the Anglican cathedral at the other end of the street. It was too expensive to complete.

1847
Irish Catholics came to Liverpool after potato famine
1856
Work began on cathedral; never completed
1922
Second building fund started
1930
Cathedral site purchased
1933
Building began to Sir Edwin Lutyens' design
1960
Competition held for more economical design
1962
Building started to Sir Frederick Gibberd's design
1967
New cathedral consecrated
1982
Mass celebrated by Pope John Paul II

After Henry VIII closed down monasteries in the 16th century, there were many laws which made practice of the Roman Catholic faith difficult in England. In 1829 the laws were changed. During the next 25 years many Catholics from Ireland emigrated to Liverpool because their potato crop failed. This was their livelihood and they needed new jobs. They wanted a cathedral to worship in.

A cathedral was designed in 1853 but only the Lady Chapel was built. In 1930 another site was bought and an enormous domed cathedral was designed by Sir Edwin Lutyens. Building stopped at the beginning of the Second World War in 1939. Only the crypt had been completed. By 1959 it was decided that it would be too expensive to build in brick and stone and that it would take too long. A competition for a new design was held and it was won by Sir Frederick Gibberd. The cathedral took less than five years to build and was consecrated in 1967.

The Metropolitan Cathedral of Christ the King is very different. It is circular and has been called 'Paddy's Wigwam' because of its tent-like appearance. It is made of steel, reinforced concrete, fibre-glass and other modern materials. The outstanding feature is to 2,000-ton lantern tower with coloured glass. It is directly above the High Altar. The altar is in the centre and is a solid block of white marble from Yugoslavia. Round it are seats for 2,300 people and everyone can see what is happening at the altar during Mass.

It is a modern cathedral. The bells are named after Matthew, Mark, Luke and John, and are electrically operated. There is even an underground car park.

1 The exterior of the circular cathedral, showing the tower which is immediately above the High Altar.

2 His Holiness Pope John Paul II celebrated Mass in the Cathedral on 30 May 1982. He also prayed in the Anglican cathedral.

36

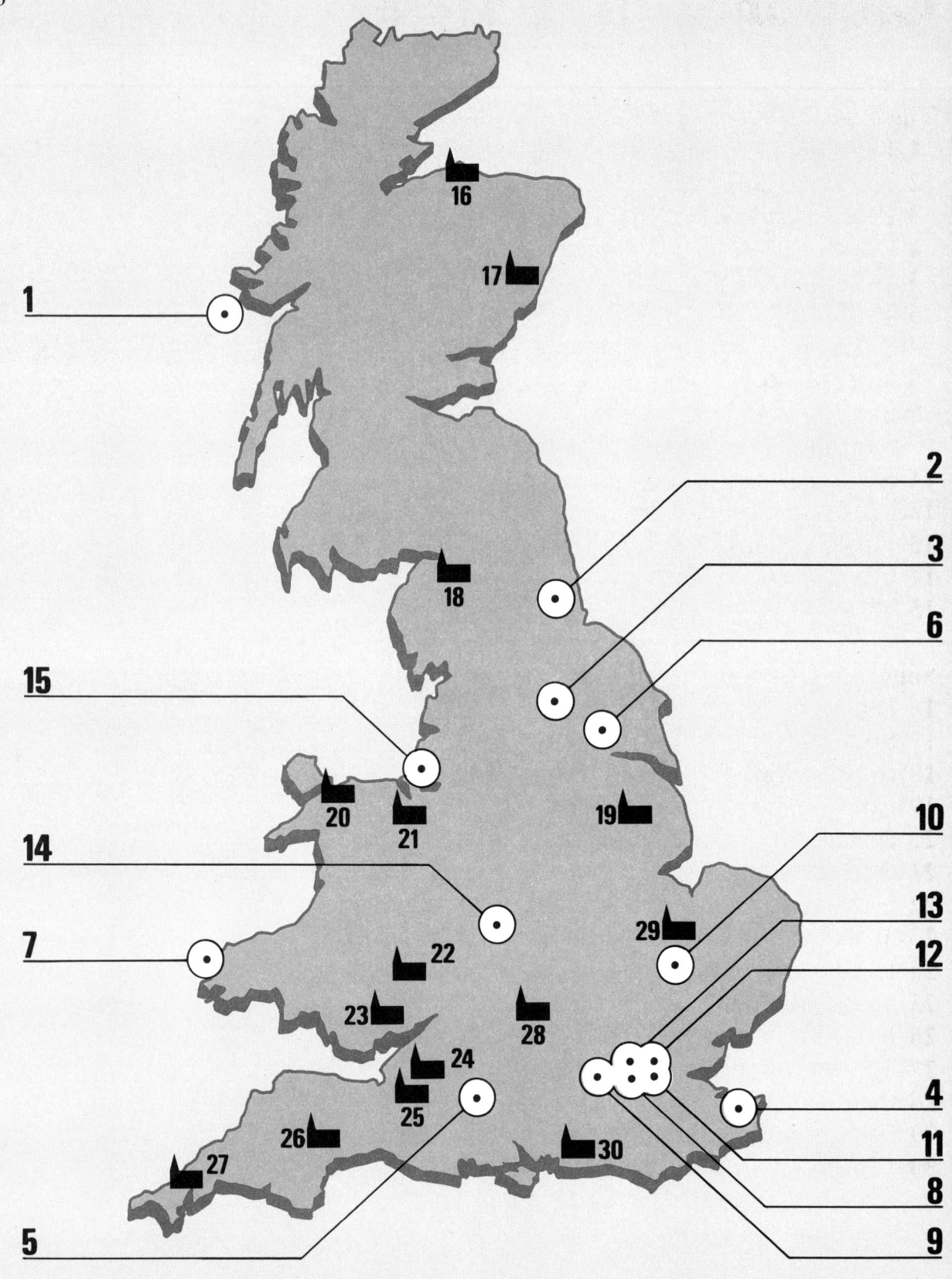

Churches of interest

The churches in this book
1 Iona, Strathclyde
2 Durham Cathedral, Durham
3 Fountains Abbey, North Yorkshire
4 Canterbury Cathedral, Kent
5 Salisbury Cathedral, Wiltshire
6 York Minster, North Yorkshire
7 St David's Cathedral, Dyfed
8 Westminster Abbey, London
9 St George's Chapel, Windsor, Berkshire
10 King's College Chapel, Cambridge
11 St Paul's Cathedral, London
12 Wesley's Chapel, City Road, London
13 Westminster Cathedral, London
14 Coventry Cathedral, Midlands
15 Metropolitan Cathedral, Liverpool

Some other interesting churches
16 Elgin Cathedral, Grampian
17 St Andrew's Cathedral, Fife
18 Carlisle Cathedral, Cumbria
19 Lincoln Cathedral, Lincolnshire
20 Bangor Cathedral, Gwynedd
21 Chester Cathedral, Cheshire
22 Hereford Cathedral, Hereford & Worcester
23 Tintern Abbey, Gwent
24 Bath Abbey, Avon
25 Wells Cathedral, Somerset
26 Exeter Cathedral, Devon
27 Truro Cathedral, Cornwall
28 Oxford Cathedral, Oxford
29 Ely Cathedral, Cambridgeshire
30 Chichester Cathedral, West Sussex

Things to look for in a church

1 Almsbox A box, usually near the door of the church, for people to put money into it to help the poor and needy.
2 Ambry (or aumbry) A cupboard set into the wall, near the altar. It was used to store the sacred vessels.
3 Boss An ornamental carving with leaves or figures. It was used to cover the joins in a vaulted ceiling where the ribs meet.
4 Brass An engraved memorial tablet set in the floor or wall of a church.
5 Church chest It was made of wood with locks and used to keep the church records, wills of parishioners, and records of births, marriages and deaths, safe.
6 Easter Sepulchre A recess in the north wall. On Good Friday, the Host and altar cross were placed there and watched over until Easter Sunday. It signified the burial and resurrection of Christ. These are now very rare.
7 Bench end (finial or poppy head) An elaborate piece of carving, usually at the top of seats or benches and pews. Sometimes weird animals and figures were carved.
8 Font This is often one of the oldest things in a church. It is used for baptisms. They used to be deep and low so adults could stand in them. Now they are shallow and raised on pedestals since sprinkling came into fashion.

9 Gargoyle A carving in the form of a grotesque face or creature sticking out from the wall. It was a water spout, designed to allow rainwater to fall away from the building.

10 Hatchment A diamond-shaped painting showing the coat of arms on a black background. These were displayed in the home after the death of a person and later placed in the church.

11 Lectern A reading desk, now used to hold the Bible when lessons are read in church. Many brass lecterns had eagles to symbolise the Gospels being carried to the four corners of the earth on their wings.

12 Lych gate (or lich gate) A gate with a roof leading to the churchyard. The coffin was rested there while the priest said part of the service.

13 Misericord A carving on the underside of a hinged choir stall. They were often humorous or grotesque. They jutted out a little so they gave some support when people had to stand for a long time.

14 Niche with saint Many churches had a niche carved from stone. It was usually outside and above the porch and had a statue of the church's patron saint in it.

15 Pulpit A raised platform from where the sermon is preached in the church. It usually has a barrier round it and is sometimes carved from stone.

16 Rood screen This was usually a very elaborately carved screen separating the chancel, which was reserved for priests, from the rest of the church. At the top, it held the crucifix (rood) and statues of the Virgin Mary and St John.

Useful addresses

English Heritage
PO Box 43
Ruislip
Middlesex HA4 0XW
(Historic Buildings and Monuments Commission)
(Written enquiries only)

The National Trust
(for Places of Historic Interest or Natural Beauty)
36 Queen Anne's Gate
London SW1H 9AS
Tel: 01 222 9251

Society for the Protection of Ancient Buildings
37 Spital Square
London E1 6DY
Tel: 01 377 1644

English Tourist Board
4 Grosvenor Gardens
London SW1W 0DJ
Tel: 01 730 3400

Scottish Tourist Board
23 Ravelston Terrace
Edinburgh EH4 3EU
Tel: 031 332 2433

National Trust for Scotland
5 Charlotte Square
Edinburgh EH2 4DU
Tel: 031 226 5922

CADW Welsh Historic Monuments/Wales Tourist Board
Brunel House
2 Fitzalan Road
Cardiff CF2 1UY
Tel: 0222 499909

Northern Ireland Tourist Board
River House
48 High Street
Belfast BT1 2DS
Tel: 0232 231221

Council for the Care of Churches
83 London Wall
London EC2M 5NA
Tel: 01 638 0971

Index

Becket, St Thomas, 12-13
Bentley, John Francis, 30
Bishop's Throne, St David's Cathedral, 19
Black Prince, 12, 13
Cambridge, 24
Canterbury Cathedral, 12-13
Canterbury Tales, 12
Catholic (see Roman Catholic)
Chaucer, Geoffrey, 12
Choir screen, York Minster, 17
Christ the King, Metropolitan Cathedral of, 34-35
Churchill, Sir Winston, 27
City Road, London, 29
Clock mechanism, 14th century, 15
Coronation Chair, 21
Coventry Cathedral, 32-33
Cromwell, Oliver, 9
Dewi Sant (see St David)
Druids, 6
Duncan, King of Scotland, 6
Durham Cathedral, 8-9
Eboracum, 16
Edward the Black Prince, 12, 13
Edward the Confessor, 20
Edward I, King, 21
Edward III, King, 22
Edward IV, King, 22
Edward V, King, 20
Edward VIII, King, 20
Edwin, King of Northumbria, 16
Elias of Dereham, Canon, 14
Elizabeth I, Queen, 21
Elizabeth II, Queen, 20, 29
Epstein, Sir Jacob, 32, 33
Ethelbert, King, 12
Eton College, 24
Festival of Nine Lessons and Carols, 24
Fire of London, the Great, 26-27
Fountains Abbey, 10-11
Garter, Order of the, 22
Garter Service, 22-23
George III, King, 29
Gibberd, Sir Frederick, 34
Godiva, Lady, 32
Gray, Walter de (see Walter de Gray)
Henry II, King, 12, 18
Henry III, King, 17, 20, 22

Henry IV, King, 13
Henry VI, King, 24
Henry VII, King, 22-23, 24
Henry VIII, King, 13, 23, 24, 30, 32, 34
Henry VII's Chapel, Westminster, 21, 24
Hutton, John, 33
Iona, 6-7
Iona Community, 7
Ireland, Kings of, 6
Joan of Navarre, 13
John Paul II, Pope, 35
King's College Chapel, 24-25
Knights of the Garter, 22
Lanfranc, Archbishop, 12
Leofric, Earl, 32
Lindisfarne, 8
Liverpool Metropolitan Cathedral, 34-35
Lutyens, Sir Edwin, 34
Macbeth, King of Scotland, 6
Magna Carta, 15
Manning, Cardinal, 30
Margaret, Queen of Scotland, 7
Methodism, 28-29
Metropolitan Cathedral, Liverpool, 34-35
Misericord, St David's Cathedral, 19
Mosaics, 31
Nash, John, 19
Nelson, Admiral Horatio, 27
Nicholas of Ely, 14
Norway, Kings of, 6
'Paddy's Wigwam', 35
Parts of a church, 4-5
Pectoral cross of St Cuthbert, 8
Philip, Prince, 29
Piper, John, 32, 33
Poets' Corner, 21
Pope John Paul II, 35
Reyntiens, Patrick, 32
Roman Catholic faith, 30-31, 34
Royal Family, 22
Rubens' The Adoration of the Magi, 24
St Augustine, 12
St Columba, 6-7
St Cuthbert, 8
St David, 18
St David's Cathedral, 18-19
St George's Chapel, 22-23, 24

St Martin's Cross, Iona, 6
St Mary's Abbey, York, 10
St Mary's Cathedral Church, Iona, 7
St Michael's Cathedral, Coventry, 32-33
St Oran's Chapel, 7
St Paul's Cathedral, 26-27
St Peter, statue of, 31
St Thomas Becket, 12-13
Salisbury Cathedral, 14-15
Sanctuary Knocker, Durham, 9
Sarum, New and Old, 14
Scotland, Kings of, 6
Scott, Sir George Gilbert, 19
Spence, Sir Basil, 32
Star of the Most Noble Order of the Garter, 22
Stone of Scone, 21
Studley Royal, 11
Sutherland, Graham, 33
Thornhill, James, 27
Unknown Warrior, Tomb of the, 21
Vaughan, Cardinal, 30
Victoria, Queen, 23
Vikings, 6-7
Walter de Gray, Archbishop of York, 16, 17
Wellington, Duke of, 27
Wesley, John, 28-29
Wesley's Chapel, 28-29
Westminster Abbey, 20-21
Westminster Cathedral, 30-31
Whispering Gallery, 27
William the Conqueror, 18, 20
William the Englishman, 12
William of Sens, 12
Windsor Castle, 22-23
Wiseman, Cardinal, 30
Wren, Sir Christopher, 27
York, Dean of, 11
York Minster, 16-17

HOUSES

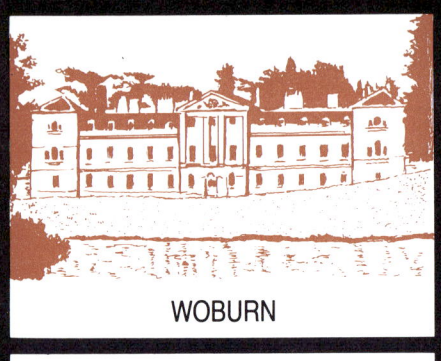

WOBURN	HAMPTON COURT	BEAULIEU
BURGHLEY	LONGLEAT	HATFIELD
HOLYROODHOUSE	CASTLE HOWARD	BLENHEIM
BROADLANDS	CHISWICK	10 DOWNING STREET
HAREWOOD	ROYAL PAVILION	BUCKINGHAM PALACE

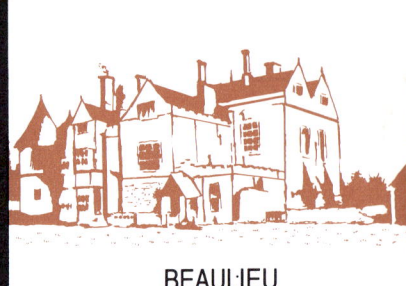

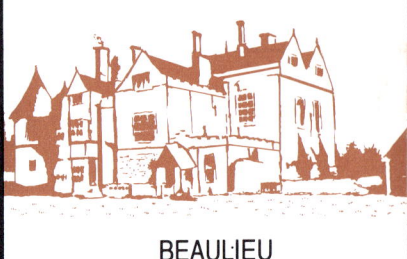

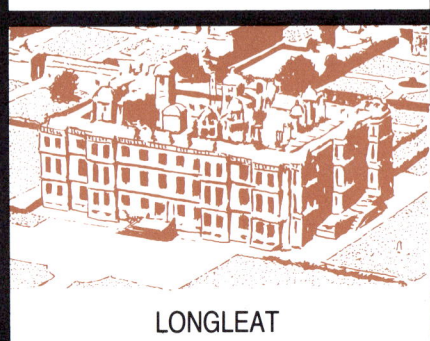

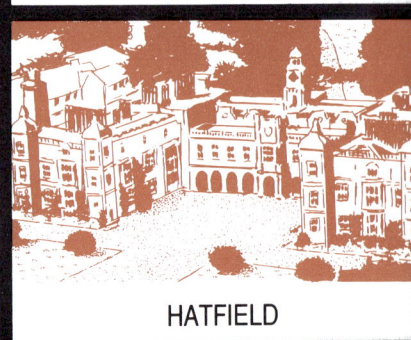

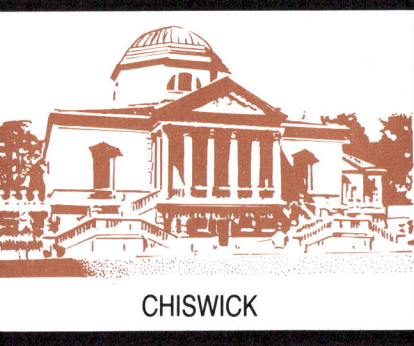

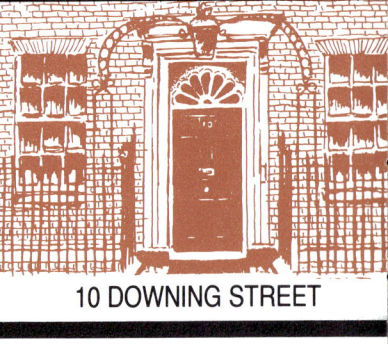

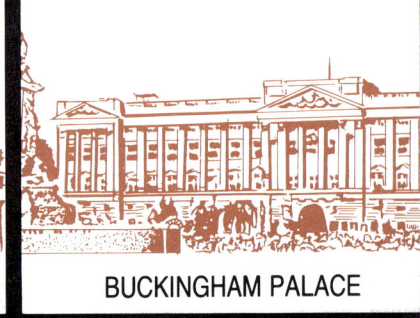